YOU ARE MIGHTY

— A GUIDE TO — CHANGING *the* WORLD

Also by Caroline Paul

The Gutsy Girl: Escapades for Your Life of Epic Adventure
(illustrated by Wendy MacNaughton)

YOU ARE MIGHTY

— A GUIDE TO —
CHANGING *the* WORLD

CAROLINE PAUL
NEW YORK TIMES Bestselling Author

ILLUSTRATED BY
LAUREN TAMAKI

BLOOMSBURY
CHILDREN'S BOOKS
LONDON   OXFORD   NEW YORK   NEW DELHI   SYDNEY

BLOOMSBURY CHILDREN'S BOOKS
Bloomsbury Publishing Plc
50 Bedford Square, London, WC1B 3DP, UK

BLOOMSBURY, BLOOMSBURY CHILDREN'S BOOKS and the Diana logo are trademarks of
Bloomsbury Publishing Plc

First published in May 2018 in the USA by Bloomsbury Children's Books
First published in Great Britain in 2019

A catalogue record for this book is available from the British Library

ISBN: 9781526602428

2 4 6 8 10 9 7 5 3 1

Printed in China by Leo Paper Products, Heshan, Guangdong

To find out more about our authors and books visit www.bloomsbury.com and sign up for our newsletters

TO MY MOM, THE FIRST ACTIVIST
IN MY LIFE

CONTENTS

A NOTE FROM THE AUTHOR

Dear Reader,

Kids have the power to change the world.

I know this isn't a surprise to you. After all, you've been standing up for what you like and what you don't since you could talk (maybe even before, if you shouted loud enough). You've been saying no (to haircuts, vitamins, long car trips) and yes (to ice cream, puppies, those cool sneakers) for pretty much your whole life. You're excellent at it.

So, what if you used the same skills that you've honed to change your world into changing *the* world?

Malala Yousafzai of Pakistan won the Nobel Peace Prize at age seventeen, and the announcement of her win probably knocked the socks off many adults. But why were they surprised? Malala began fighting for the rights of girls just like her when she was just eleven years old. She said

no (to oppression) and yes (to education for girls), speaking up about right and wrong, justice and injustice, despite death threats and even an attempt on her life! As you can see, this isn't about haircuts and cool clothes. This is superhero stuff. But Malala, despite her integrity and dazzling courage, is merely human, so we don't call her a superhero.

We call her an activist.

This book doesn't tell you what to stand up for, or against. Nor does it define right and wrong, because you have a good sense of that already. What this book does is offer much of what you'll need in your own quest for justice. (Except the cape. That you will have to obtain on your own.)

Thank you in advance for changing the world.

Sincerely,

Carolia

Caroline Paul
(The Author)

FIEFDOMS, MIDDLE AGES

SUFFRAGETTES, 1900S

CIVIL RIGHTS, 1960S

VIETNAM WAR, 1970S

SAVE THE WHALES (ONGOING)

ARMS RACE, 1980S

QUEER RIGHTS, 2000S

PEACE ON MARS, 3012

INTRODUCTION

Welcome to this how-to manual on being an activist. You've opened these pages because you are on a quest to change the world. And there is no better time to do it than NOW.

You may be angry about an injustice. You may be scared about a situation you've just heard about. You may be excited to support a cause you believe in. All these feelings are normal. What's more, these feelings are *powerful*.

This book will help channel your emotions into action. It offers a simple list of tactics used to great effect by kids just like you. Their stories are not only inspiring but instructive. They identified an issue they cared about. They researched that issue, enlisted friends, parents, and strangers to their cause, and made a plan. Then they acted!

This book also includes concepts vital for your tactics to work, like privilege, intersectionality, and escalation, among others. If you're thinking, "Whoa, those are long complicated words," remember that "vacation" and "chocolatefudgesundae" are pretty long words, too. So don't be intimidated. Having a good grasp of these ideas and how they apply to you and your cause is key to changing the world for the better.

Now, gather your friends (because world-changing doesn't happen alone), turn the page, and read about tactics that have made a difference before and will make a difference again, with you!

1) CHANGE YOUR HABITS

Sometimes saving the world begins with the smallest of actions: a tiny tweak to your own daily life.

This is what **Merit Leighton**, six, and **Marlowe Peyton**, four, decided to do when they learned about the horrifying amount of plastic rubbish in the Pacific Ocean. Calling themselves the Plastic Patrol, they collected and recycled discarded plastic bottles from the beach, refused plastic straws in their drinks, and turned down plastic takeaway utensils!

You may think that cutting down on your plastic use won't do much. But Americans purchase over *fifty billion* (yes, with a *b*) plastic bottles a year and recycle less than half of those. Annually we EACH throw away about 84 kilos of plastic. Much of it ends up in the ocean, where it waits to degrade. How long until it's good and gone? Up to a thousand years. Meanwhile marine animals mistakenly eat it; this poisons them or blocks their digestive tracts, starving them. The plastic also breaks into microscopic pieces that congregate in sea currents. In sum, millions of dolphins, turtles, and fish die each year, and we are stuck with polluted gyres like the Great Pacific Garbage Patch, floating with a gazillion (yes, with a *g*!!!) tiny plastic particles, all because we keep carelessly using and then throwing away bottles, bags, balloons, and straws, among many other things.

Your habit change extends beyond your own daily life. When friends and family observed Merit and Marlowe, it gave them a chance to think about the plastic in their own lives. This may have inspired them to also cut back on plastic. And still more people may have been inspired by those people. Think of it: ultimately one person's action could lead to a resolution to cut out plastic *by the whole entire world*. I know that sounds improbable, but to activists "improbable" sounds like "totally freaking possible."

Genesis Palacio was just three years old when she asked her mum where chicken nuggets came from, and her mum had to break it to her: animals are killed for her food. Genesis was shocked and saddened. Animals? For food? She told her mum she no longer wanted chicken nuggets, or any other meat. Within a year, the entire Palacio family became vegetarian, too!

Genesis wanted to save animals, but it turns out she was also saving the planet, because raising animals to eat requires a lot of water, a lot of land, and a lot of pollutants like petrol, diesel, and coal. Something as simple as eating less meat is a powerful way to help the earth. Not to mention that you will make a tree, a stream, and a super cute pig very happy.

Genesis eventually became a vegan, which means she cut all animal products from her diet. When she munches on just one peanut butter and jelly sandwich instead of a hamburger, she helps save the life of one cow as well as more than 1.5 kilos of greenhouse gases, 1,000 litres of water, and from one to five square metres of land.

VS

EATING 1 PEANUT BUTTER & JELLY SANDWICH SAVES

1.5 KILOS OF GREENHOUSE GAS

1,000 LITRES OF WATER

ONE TO FIVE SQUARE METRES OF LAND

1 COW'S LIFE

WORKBOOK

1. What's your concern?

2. Brainstorm what small daily action could influence that issue. If it's animal welfare, you might decide to eliminate meat and dairy. If it's the environment, cut out paper towels (use a sponge!) or paper napkins (use cloth!). Maybe you'll take your own bag to the supermarket. Get a bunch of friends together and brainstorm. Then make these changes together!

3. Can you measure what impact your action is having? (If you go to the shop four times a week and bring your own bag, how many plastic bags are you NOT using?) If your action is creating change, keep going. If you want to make an even bigger impact, tweak another habit!

4. Repeat steps 2 and 3. Get more friends on board!

2) MAKE A PROTEST SIGN

Sometimes the best way to communicate your support, or your concern, is to hold up a big sign with a message on it.

As you can see, these messages are short and clear. There isn't a lot of space on your poster, and you want your message to be seen and understood! This is why you shouldn't write this:

YOU KNOW WHAT, I'M JUST NOT SO
SURE I LIKE WHAT'S GOING ON WITH THE
AIR AND THE WATER AND THE TREES
(NOT TO MENTION THE POLAR BEARS!),
BECAUSE IT JUST SORT OF REALLY, REALLY
MAKES ME MAD.

Cora Colin, eight, was saddened by the election of US president Donald Trump. "He wants to build a wall between our country and Mexico. But he's not the boss of where people go!" So Cora drew a sign that read **Build Bridges, Not Walls**. She used the sign in a protest march (see **March** on page 86) with her family, but she also held it up to the car window as they drove there and back, so that people in passing vehicles and on pavements could think about her slogan. "Bridges connect people and walls separate people," she explained.

Your protest sign should make a statement (**We Shall Overcome**), support a cause (**Peace on Earth**), or ask for a change (**Stop Animal Testing**). Once you've made your sign, you can press it against the car window (like Cora did), attach a stick to it and wave it about, or prop it up outside your house (or someone else's, but that is not recommended).

WORKBOOK

Here's what you'll need to make a wise, impactful (and maybe even humorous) protest sign:

1. A cause!

2. Something to write on

3. Stick and tape (optional)

4. Something to write with

5. A sense of purpose (possibly outrage!)

6. A message

7. A good design: Big letters! Bright colours! Bold drawings!

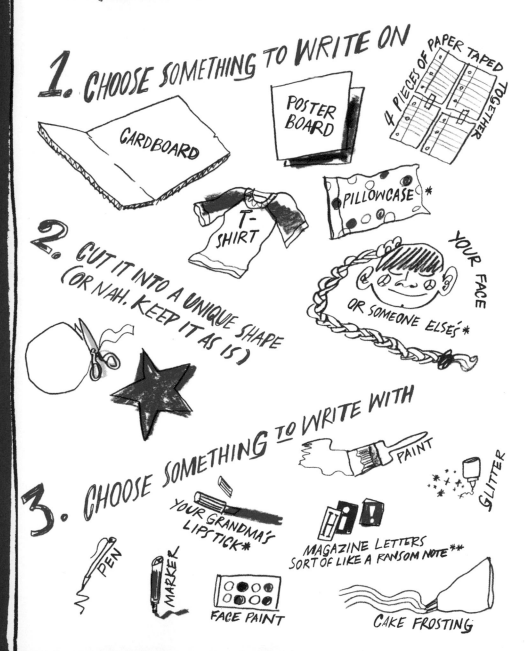

AWESOME PROTEST SIGN

4. CHOOSE SOMETHING TO SAY

MAKE SURE YOUR MESSAGE IS CLEAR

BE CATCHY! IT'S FINE TO RHYME.

REMEMBER TO "KISS" =
KEEP IT SHORT + SNAPPY
(+ SUPER SIMPLE).

DON'T USE WORDS LIKE
"ANTIDISESTABLISHMEN-
TARIANISM." ***

WHEN WORDS FAIL, ADD A PICTURE.

5. CHOOSE SOMETHING TO HOLD UP YOUR AWESOME PROTEST SIGN

LONG STICK (TAPE IT TO THE SIGN'S BACK)

BUBBLE GUM
(STICK THE SIGN AGAINST THE WALL)

STRING

(MAKE HOLES ON THE TOP 2 CORNERS, RUN STRING THROUGH, HANG AROUND YOUR NECK + SHOULDERS.)

YOUR ARM

YOUR LITTLE BROTHER'S ARM ****

***ONE OF THE LONGEST WORDS IN THE ENGLISH LANGUAGE.

**** (WITH HIM ATTACHED, OF COURSE).

3) PETITION

One of the first things we ever learn to write is our own name. This is for good reason. Our name in print is one of the ways we say, *Hey, I'm here!* A petition goes one step further. It says, *Hey, I'm here, and I have something to say!*

Ten-year-old **Mia Hansen** liked her Jamba Juice smoothies, but not the Styrofoam cups in which they were served. She knew that Styrofoam takes over a million years(!) to disappear from the earth, it contains toxic and carcinogenic chemicals, and animals eat Styrofoam litter and die. So she started a petition using an online petition site. A petition is like a letter, but instead of being signed *Sincerely yours, Just Lil' Old Me*, it is signed by a ton of people. When it came to Mia's petition, "a ton" was a whopping 130,000 names! Within three weeks of starting the petition, Jamba Juice executives contacted Mia to tell her they would switch their cups from Styrofoam to material less harmful to the environment.

Katy Butler, seventeen, started a petition when she realized that *Bully*, a documentary on bullying, might not be available to teens because it was rated R instead of PG-13. Katy, who had been bullied in middle school, knew the movie's message was vital, so she turned to an online petition site and used their platform to ask that the Motion Picture Association of America reconsider its rating. "Over 13 million kids will be bullied this year alone. Think of how many of these kids could benefit from seeing this film," the petition stated. Over 500,000 people signed, and (after a small edit of three swear words), the rating was changed to PG-13, allowing the film to be shown in schools and cinemas around the United States.

Both Katy and Mia show that petitions do work. It takes a lot of passion and commitment to put a petition together: you have to research the cause, write an explanatory paragraph, and then gather signatures, either over the internet or in person. But it doesn't take a lot of effort to sign one's name to a piece of paper. Companies and governments understand that *you* are a serious activist, but they might not think the same of your signers. This is why it is important to pair petitions with media attention and social media (see **Use Social Media** on page 52). This will spread your petition's message, and put even more pressure on those who can change the situation.

WORKBOOK

There are petitions online that you can sign, but you can start one yourself!

1. What's your cause?

2. Gather information.

3. Figure out to whom the petition should be addressed. It's all fine and good to petition your mum to sack your local MP, but I'm sad to say she just doesn't have the power. Make sure the person, company, or government you're approaching can enact the change you are demanding.

4. Enlist friends to help! Adults, too.

5. Write the statement explaining what you want and why.

6. Gather signatures. You could use an online petition site like Change.org, and spread word via social media (see **Use Social Media** on page 52). You could print out your own and set up a table outside a shop or pass it around at your school, if allowed. You can also hand out copies of the petition so that others can gather even more signatures.

7. Contact your local newspaper, television news station, and radio station and inform them of your cause and/or send a press release. Media coverage not only increases the possible number of signatures, it promotes awareness of your cause. It also convinces those you are petitioning to pay attention to you, because the last thing they want is negative media attention!

8. Send petition (see step 3).

9. Wait.

10. If there is no response to the petition, escalate! Go back to the media and update them. Consider a personal meeting (see **Speak Face-to-Face** on page 40), a demonstration (see **March** on page 86), or a sit-in (see **Just Sit Down** on page 99).

ACTIVIST TIP ESCALATE

What happens when your first efforts don't lead
to change? It's time to **escalate**.

Write a polite letter.
   No answer
Make a phone call to ask for a meeting.
   No answer
March!
   Still no answer
Sit in!
   Hey! Hi! Hello!
Can we talk?

PRESS RELEASE

Here is an example of what a press release looks like.

ATTENTION-GETTING HEADLINE

WE'RE FED UP WITH FUR!

A VERY AWESOME AND INDIGNANT PROTEST!

WHAT YOU'RE DOING

← WHEN IT WILL HAPPEN

11 AM, SATURDAY JULY 28, 2018

At the corner of Main and Smith Street

WHERE IT WILL HAPPEN

Who needs fur? No one. So ten animal lovers with a conscience are dressing up as foxes and minks and parading in front of (BIG DEPARTMENT STORE THAT SELLS FUR) **to demand an end to fur selling.**

SHORT AND RIGHTEOUS EXPLANATION OF YOUR ACTIONS!

DESCRIPTIVE PHOTO

CONTACT:

AN ADULT'S PHONE NUMBER OR EMAIL

4) VOLUNTEER!

Your time is precious. There are skateboards to ride, books to read, and cookies to eat. But your time is also POWERFUL. You can offer it up to an organization that does something awesome for the world. Are you concerned about trash on the beach? Do you think planting trees is important? There are lots of groups that need help and would welcome the energy and optimism that kids like you bring.

Savanah Blessing, fourteen, volunteers once a week at a soup kitchen that serves vegan food to people who are homeless or in need. As many as two hundred people wait in line for the meal each evening, and she finds the service a deeply fulfilling experience. "I get to see the joy on people's faces when they are handed a warm, nice plate of food," she explained.

If you can't find a place to volunteer, then you could always do what **Jonas Corona** did when he was only six years old: establish an organization yourself! Jonas wanted to help kids who were homeless, but all the places he contacted told him he was too young to volunteer. So, with the help of his parents, he started Love in the Mirror, which gathers food and clothes and distributes them to those living on the streets or in shelters or waiting for foster care placement.

WORKBOOK

1. What is the injustice that concerns you?

2. Look up organizations nearby that have experience in this area.

3. Call them or peruse their website to make sure they take child volunteers. Let them know what you're good at that would be of use to them. (You may be skilled at shooting spitballs, making fart noises, and winning Jenga, but those aren't as helpful as being kind to animals, washing lettuce and potatoes, and picking up litter.)

4. Grab a few kids from your block to come with you. Even your little sister might join (or your big sister, if you need someone to drive you). Perhaps you can convince your school to sponsor activities with that organization!

COUNT ME IN!

5) RAISE MONEY

Dough. Bread. Bacon. Breadwinner. Bring home the bacon. These are just some of the slang words and phrases we use to mean "money." Why so many food references? We humans think money is tasty stuff. And just like living creatures need food, every cause needs money in order to survive.

When ten-year-old **Miguel Billings** heard that Haiti had just been hit by a hurricane, and then learned that the country had never really recovered from a devastating earthquake six years before, he decided he would raise money to build new houses. How? With his latest skill: playing the baritone horn. But would that make money magically appear? Nope. So he came up with a plan: he knew how he would highlight his cause (play on the pavement outside his home), who would give money (the neighbours within earshot, hopefully), who would help (his little sisters, who made cookies and signs), and to whom the money would go (Lifeline Christian Mission, a charity that was already active in Haiti).

News of Miguel's fund-raiser was posted to the local neighbourhood email list, drawing even more donors. Miguel's mum eventually used a crowdfunding site to manage the donations (Kickstarter, GoFundMe, and Piggybackr are a few examples of such sites). But, as Miguel knew, posting your cause on the internet doesn't mean you can just sit back and watch the money roll in. If you walk near a chocolate factory, do chocolate bars rain down on you? Unfortunately, no. The least you have to do is ask. That's often not enough, either. This is why Miguel, who decided to raise enough money to build one house in Haiti, kept playing his baritone horn. Yes, people wanted to fork over their hard-earned pocket money because he had a good cause, but they also admired Miguel's verve and appreciated his music! Three weeks later, Miguel reached his goal.

Mikaila Ulmer was scared of bees. Who could blame her? She was four years old and had been stung twice in one week. But her mum encouraged her to learn about bees as a way to get over her fear, and so they sat down together and began their research. Mikaila soon realized that these insects were vital to our planet (many of our food crops need to be pollinated by bees to thrive), but they were in grave danger. Pesticides, poor nutrition (bee industries often feed their bees high-fructose corn syrup instead of giving them the honey they make), and viruses all account for a crashing bee population. Excited about supporting bees and beekeepers, Mikaila began to sell honey-sweetened lemonade when she was just five years old. Soon a local pizza restaurant requested it for their customers, and her drink took off. Now Mikaila's honey lemonade can be found on store shelves across the United States. The bees and beekeepers are big winners here: Mikaila buys their honey, donates to bee organizations around the world, and makes speeches on their importance and plight.

Mikaila and Miguel raised money using different methods, and they didn't just ask people for their cash; they offered something in return. What can you offer? Form a band and put on a show. Organize a scavenger hunt. Put on a rope-skipping event. Let people watch as you attempt to break the world record on the pogo stick (warning: the current record is 206,864 bounces).

Remember, it's not enough to bake brownies or sing songs. You have to research and then inform your potential donors about the issue you're raising money for. Hand over facts that stir the heart and soul; people are very willing to give money to a cause that they really understand.

WORKBOOK

1. What's your concern?

2. What organization best represents your concern?

3. Do they need money? Probably. But ask them (via email or a phone call! You can often find this contact information on the internet). If the organization is local, stop by in person!

4. Figure out how best to raise money. Brainstorm ideas: bake sale, walkathon, slam poetry performance? Will you manage the money through a crowdfunding site?

5. Gather information. Talk to someone from the organization you are supporting, or scour the internet for facts!

6. Write about your cause in a short paragraph. People need to be informed in order to be as passionate about the issue as you are (but not bored by too many reading materials)! Give your friends and neighbours good reasons to fork over their money.

7. Spread the word by email, Twitter, Snapchat, and Instagram (see **Use Social Media** on page 52). Don't forget to alert local radio stations and newspapers.

6) WRITE A LETTER

This doesn't seem very exciting. Who wants to sit down and compose words when you could be chaining yourself to an old-growth sequoia tree? But letters make a difference. Writing sincerely about your concern can have great impact. Being polite is also important (no one likes to be shouted at).

Alex Myteberi was six years old when he saw a newspaper photo of a young Syrian boy named Omran Daqdeesh wounded by an attack during his country's long civil war. The bomb had killed Omran's family. Alex immediately took out a pencil and lined yellow paper and went straight to the top with a request.

08, 21, 2010

Dear President obama,
Remember the boy who was
picked up by the ambulance in
Syria? Can you please go get
him and bring him to
                Park in the driveway or
on the street and we'll be wai-
-ting for you guys with flags
flowers and balloons. We
~~~~~~ will ~~~~ give him a
family and he will be our
brother. Catherine, my little
sister Will be collect-
-ing butterflies and fireflies
for him. In my school I have
a friend from Syria, Omar, and
I will introduce him to Omar and

We CAm all PlAy together.
We can invite him to birthday
Parties and he will teach us anoth
-er language. We can teach him Eng
-lish too, Just like we taught my
friend Aoto from Japan. Please tell him
that his brother will be Alex
Who is a very kind boy, Just like
him. Since he won't bring toys and
doesn't have toys Catherine will
Share her big blue stripy white
bunny. And I Will Share my
bikke and I Will teach him
how to ride it. I Will teach
him additions and Subtraction
in math. and he Smell Catherine
's lip gloss penguin which is

green. She doesn't let anyone
touch it.

Thank you very much! I CAn't
Wait for you to come!

Alex
6 years old

Omran did not move to Alex's home. But the letter was read by President Obama at an international summit on the worldwide refugee crisis, and many influential people heard Alex's words. Millions also read the letter on the internet after it was posted there by the White House. Alex's generosity most likely inspired people to consider the plight of war refugees. Maybe his action showed that standing up against the brutal Syrian conflict was possible. Perhaps his kindness encouraged others to be kinder. All these are awesome reasons to sit down and put your concerns into words.

In 1982, **Samantha Smith**, ten, was worried about nuclear weapons, which were being manufactured at an alarming pace in both the Soviet Union and the United States. At the time, the two countries considered themselves mortal enemies. So Samantha wrote a letter to the new president of the Soviet Union, Yuri Andropov. She congratulated him on his new job (politeness!), explained she was very worried about nuclear war, and then asked him whether he would be launching missiles at the United States.

"If you aren't please tell me how you are going to help to not have a war," she wrote.

And he wrote back! In his long letter, President Andropov assured her that he and his country wanted peace as much as she did. He explained that Russia wanted to do anything they could to avoid a terrible war.

Their correspondence ignited media attention, and soon the citizens of both countries were captivated. Samantha was invited to the Soviet Union, and in turn, a few years later, an eleven-year-old Russian named **Katya Lycheva** visited America. These exchanges were discussed in schools, in homes, and on city streets. While it is difficult to calibrate the exact impact of Samantha's letter, her gesture and President Andropov's thoughtful reply humanized both countries, and diffused some of the sinister perceptions each had of the other.

The letter you write might not elicit the personal responses that both Samantha and Alex received. Instead the sentences will be mealymouthed and vague, and upon close inspection the signature won't be from a pen, but from a stamp. This is called a "form letter" because the same letter is used to respond to anyone who writes. Even more disappointing, sometimes you do not get a response at all! But this doesn't mean your voice has not been heard. Someone has opened your letter and noted your concern – and when a lot of people write with that same concern, change can come (see **Go to It!** on page 106).

By the way, there are many different ways to contact leaders these days. You can tweet, you can post on Facebook, and you can phone. But studies show that both personal emails and handwritten letters are some of the best ways to communicate with an elected official. The only better way (according to the Congressional Management Foundation, and it sounds like they should know) is to meet that leader in person (see **Speak Face-to-Face** on page 40)!

WORKBOOK

1. Determine which people are directly involved in your concern. (Is it the head of a company? Is it someone in the media?) Find their addresses using the internet or a smart adult!

2. Be precise in your writing and requests. No need to challenge someone to an arm-wrestling match or use disrespectful language. People respond best to well-thought-out arguments and sincere personal stories.

3. While you're at it, be sure to get in touch with those who represent your area in Parliament. This is a powerful way to effect change! Your MP is there in Parliament to stand for you and your family. To find out who your MP is and how to contact him or her, go to www.parliament. uk/get-involved/contact-your-mp/ (in the UK) or www.australia.gov.au/ about-government/contact-government/contact-ministers-members-and-senators (in Australia).

While you're at it, don't forget to write a letter to the head honcho.

In the UK
The Prime Minister
Office of the Prime Minister
10 Downing Street
London SW1A 2AA

In Australia
Prime Minister
Parliament House
Canberra
ACT 2600

ACTIVIST TIP **BE AN ALLY**

What if you're concerned about the bullying of your gay friends, but you yourself are straight? What if you're outraged about police brutality against the black community, but you yourself are white? In other words, what if you are not directly affected by the injustice at hand, but you want to fight that injustice? Your job is not to speak on behalf of these friends and family members. Your job is to support. In other words, sometimes the most powerful activism you can do is to be the great kid behind the great kid. This is called being an ally.

1. Listen to people who directly experience the injustice.

2. Believe your friend when they tell you about their experiences of discomfort and outright prejudice.

3. Ask "How can I be helpful?"

4. Accept that there is lots you don't know about issues you don't experience firsthand (even if you think you do).

5. Especially if you think you do.

6. Spread the word of a friend's cause on your social media feeds.

7. Say no to comments about kids of other races.

8. As a boy, say no to sexist comments made by other boys.

9. As a straight kid, say no to homophobic comments made by other straight kids.

10. As a cis-gendered kid, say no to transphobic comments made by other cis-gendered kids.

11. In fact, speak out and say no to anyone ridiculing any group.

12. Learn about the issue.

13. Stand behind your friend. Literally, behind.

14. Apologize if you misstep. We all misstep.

15. Did we mention Listen More? *We can't say it enough*. Listen More, more.

16. Commit to doing better.

7) SPEAK FACE-TO-FACE

Texting is fun. So is Skype. And, soon, holograms! But we're human, not robots, and ultimately IRL is still the most effective invention around.

This is why when a young black man was shot by police in Charlotte, North Carolina, nine-year-old **Zianna Oliphant** attended the emergency town council meeting, walked to the podium, and addressed the mayor of Charlotte. "We are black people, and we shouldn't have to feel like this," she said. "We shouldn't have to protest. . . We do this because we need to and have rights. . . It's a shame that our fathers and mothers are killed, and we can't even see them any more. . . We have tears, and we shouldn't have tears. We need our fathers and mothers to be by our side."

The room was electrified. And no wonder: Zianna was authentic and passionate. She was also speaking face-to-face to someone in charge, and that is powerful. We're human after all, and looking another person in the eye – even someone who may disagree with you – is the most effective way to make a connection and be remembered. Okay, you're not old enough to vote. But elected officials know that you hold sway with your parents and other adults, and *they* vote. So your presence at a political meeting carries weight. You can speak at the podium, like Zianna did, or if you're shy, sit in the front row and hold a sign (see **Make a Protest Sign** on page 8). Even better: arrange a meeting at your local councillor/MP's office. Call or email using information you can find online.

The powerful person you need to meet may not reside in government. This person may be the head of a global company, or the president of the union, or the head of your local school board . . . or your school headteacher. The advice is the same – once you get a meeting, prepare yourself well! Be polite. And get a clear answer to your question/request before you leave.

WORKBOOK

1. You're concerned about an issue – find the person who has the power to make change. Is it your mayor? Your local councillor? The school board? Your MP? The head of a company?

2. What is the best way to meet face-to-face? Is it at a public meeting or at their offices?

3. If it's at a meeting, find out when the next one is. If it's at an office, make an appointment!

4. Research your issue well.

5. Write down what you're going to say when asking for an appointment. Here is a sample script (good for both phone or email).

Dear (Person in power),

I am concerned about (issue here). I believe that you can help change the situation by (solution you've come up with here). I would like to speak to you face-to-face. I am able to meet you after school. What day works for you?

**Sincerely yours,
(You)**

6. If you're like most of us, your mind will go blank when you are faced with an audience. So have your points prepared! You've done your research (see step 4); it's time to organize your thoughts and write them down. Gather a group of friends to help you.

7. Once you're in the meeting or office, you need to speak! First, state the major problem – in Zianna's case it was racial prejudice among law enforcement. Then either ask what will be done or, better yet, offer up the solution yourself.

8. Leave the meeting with a sense of how the problem will be solved, and follow up quickly with an email to make sure it happens. If you see no changes, escalate!

ACTIVIST TIP PRIVILEGE

Ah, cake. How satisfying to take a few steps, reach out, and grab it when you want it. But what if your friend, who also loves cake, can't get to it so easily? Instead, she must slog up a steep stairway full of treacherous obstacles. Only then is the cake available to her. Yet neither of you deserved the cake more than the other.

If you are born with traits the world has traditionally valued – like skin colour (if it's white); gender (if it's male); sexual orientation (if it's straight); physical and mental health; access to wealth; and a cisgender identity, among others – life can be more of a short, shallow ramp to access the things you want or need. This is what it is like to have privilege. The world respects, protects, and promotes people with privilege in ways big and small, daily.

Why is this important? Because sometimes what a person says is unjust may not seem like a big deal to you. But consider: have you simply been shielded from this injustice by your privileged traits? It can be hard to see at first, because privilege is often invisible to those who have it.

For example, if you are white, you may not notice that many television shows, books, and movies feature white families. It can be hard to see the flip side: that a black, brown, or mixed-race kid, who can't find media that reflects his experience, will feel unsupported by the world around him. Similarly, if you are an able-bodied kid, you may not think much about the

stairs that lead to your classroom. But for your friend, one with a disability that makes it difficult or impossible to navigate steps, the school day will be harder. To get to maths class, a ramp will need to be found or a longer, more circuitous route followed.

What if you were not born with traits that offer privilege? Perhaps you are brown, you are female, you have a disability, you are gender nonconforming, or you are queer, among others? These traits are awesome. But they have been wrongly devalued during hundreds (or thousands!) of years of racism, sexism, and classism. Your journey will be different from those with privileged traits; it may be difficult in ways big and small, daily, because you live in a culture that has a long history of throwing treacherous obstacles your way. Why is this important? You will experience injustices that your friends may not seem to get. But your experience is real, and it is a powerful indicator of master forces at work that both those activists with privilege and those without must conquer. You are an important voice in the fight for an equitable world.

So ask: how much privilege do you experience in your daily life? Privilege can be found in things like your physical health, nationality, immigration status, gender orientation, sexual orientation, mental health, gender, religion, race, physical looks, wealth, and education, to name a few! Sometimes it's not crystal clear – a white girl has privilege in some areas but not in others. Ditto for a Mexican American boy (see **Intersectionality** on page 68 for more).

If you don't understand the forces that advantage you, you are often upholding the very injustices you are trying to change! But once you understand your privileges, you can use this knowledge to be a better activist against this unfair system (see **Be an Ally** on page 38).

8) BOYCOTT

Have you heard the expression "money talks"? This doesn't mean that money says things like *Hey, what's up?* It means money sends a powerful message. So if a company or a product is in any way harming the world, tell them what you think about that by refusing to give them your pocket money. That's boycotting. And tell everyone you know to do the same. That's called organizing a boycott!

Boycotts are powerful because a company's first concern is their profit. If you don't spend your money on their products, their profit goes down. Then they start to listen, and possibly change. When a company changes its ways in response to a boycott, it may release a statement that says, *Oh, yes, we realize how wrong we were to (test on animals/pay tiny wages/manufacture harmful products)*. This apology is satisfying, but don't let up on your boycott until you have seen the actual change you want!

It's important to pair a boycott with a clear request. This is what **students at Roosevelt High School** in Chicago did. Their school lunches consisted of rotten fruit, stale bread, and undercooked meat! The students organized – which means they came together as a group behind a single goal – and boycotted the food company by refusing the inedible meals. They knew that this would send a clear message to the school headteacher and the school board. Then the students demanded a specific result. "We want bigger portions, more nutritious food, and (food) partly handmade from scratch," student **Shirley Hernandez** told the media who covered the event.

By the way, this boycott was not just about bad meals. The students were being devalued because they were from poor neighbourhoods. They united to show that this did not mean that they were disempowered!

Like many boycotts, this one took aim at profit; the food (if you could call it food) company lost money on every meal that wasn't served.

WORKBOOK

1. Your goal is to change policy within a company by hitting them where it hurts. No, not THERE. In the wallet! You want to stop the company from earning money. This means you stop buying their goods and you make sure as many other people as possible do so, too. What company are you targeting?

2. Research exactly what the company is doing wrong!

3. Contact the company and inform it of your impending boycott. Tell them that they can stop the boycott by stopping the injustice they're involved in. Who knows, they might crumble then and there.

4. Enlist your friends to join you.

5. Escalate! Write a press release about what you're doing and why, and send it to newspapers, magazines, and bloggers.

6. Keep escalating! Broadcast your intentions all over social media (see **Use Social Media** on page 52). The more people who boycott, the more money the company will lose, and the more they are likely to listen. Still, companies have what are called "deep pockets," which means a lot of money resides there. Keep boycotting! Even if policy doesn't change, you are making a statement, and people are hearing it (see **Go to It!** on page 106).

9) USE SOCIAL MEDIA

You may be highly skilled at posting on Twitter, Snapchat, and Instagram. But the way you use social media for a cause is different from the way you use it with your friends. This is not about photos of your kitten, even if your kitten is ridiculously cute.

The Dakota Access pipeline carrying oil from North Dakota to Illinois, in the United States, was supposed to cross Bismark, North Dakota. But the citizens there (who are mostly white) objected, so it was rerouted toward the Sioux Standing Rock Reservation. Like those in Bismark, thirteen-year-old **Tokata Iron Eyes** and her friends feared that the pipeline would endanger their water and sully their land (there were three hundred reported breaks in other pipelines around North Dakota in just one year). They decided to start a petition (see **Petition** on page 14). Using their social media feeds, they spread news of this petition far and wide, with hashtags such as #NoDAPL and #Rezpectourwater. Once they had gathered enough signatures, they ran a three-thousand-kilometre relay race to deliver that petition and its message to Congress and the Army Corps of Engineers. This, too, was covered on YouTube, Facebook, and on the Standing Rock Kids Twitter feed, @ReZpectOurWater. When it was announced that construction would begin anyway, activists of all ages set up an encampment to block the

TYPE
-TYPE

work, and the young people tweeted, Facebooked, and Instagrammed from there. When police sprayed tear gas and released attack dogs, Facebook Live captured the scene, which shocked the world and raised even more awareness.

What the youth of Standing Rock understood was that social media is a powerful "amplifier." Technically an amplifier is a box that raises the volume of a musical instrument for concert fans seated in the last row. Likewise social media sharing raises the volume of a cause, so that a wider audience can hear it. But like an amplifier needs an electric guitar, social media needs an action. This is why the Standing Rock kids did more than type on their phones. They initiated that petition, organized that run, and also lived at the protest encampment, using social media to communicate their actions, and the results, to the world.

WORKBOOK

1. Is social media a good way to amplify your cause, and if so what platforms will you use? The youth of the Standing Rock reservation used Twitter and Facebook to spread the word about their petition, their run, and their encampment.

2. Will you be changing the message depending on the platform? The Native American youth against the Dakota Access pipeline varied their approach; some tweeted about the petition, but others made videos that encouraged people to follow them on social media.

3. Brainstorm key allies who will help spread the word on their own social media platforms. It may be an author who has written a book about these issues. It might be a celebrity who regularly speaks out about your cause. It could be your mum, if your mum has a huge following! Don't forget to go old-fashioned and connect with the social media platforms of various media outlets. Tell them all what's going on!

4. What is your goal with social media amplification? For the Standing Rock kids, it was to gain signatures for their petition, and alert the public to dangers of a pipeline near their water and sacred land.

10) SHOOT A VIDEO

Everyone loves to sit down to a good web TV show. So why not write, shoot, edit, and then post one yourself?

Robby Novak was nine years old when he took on the role of Kid President. He and his (adult) brother-in-law teamed up to film Robby's inspirational speeches on how he, as president, would "make the world awesome," and how we can do that, too. His advice includes Twenty Things We Should Say More Often ("Thank you," "I don't know," "Here is a surprise corn dog I bought you because you are my friend") and how we should dance more, stop being boring, and if two roads diverge in a yellow wood, definitely pick the "one that leads to awesome." The first video was posted on the internet and watched by friends and family, but it quickly spread, and now the series is followed by tens of millions of people. Robby's message about justice is simple: be nice and respectful to yourself and others.

When **Jazz Jennings** was born, people said she was a boy. But as soon as she was old enough to have the words, she let everyone know that she was actually a girl. So at age six, with her parents' help, she set about living her life as she truly was, dressing as a girl, taking hormones to allow her to develop as a girl, and identifying publicly as a girl. To those who are cis-gender (the gender you were assigned at birth matches your gender identity), being transgender (the gender you were assigned at birth does not match your gender identity) is often confounding. Trans people are also subject to prejudice and violence. So Jazz made videos on her YouTube channel, I Am Jazz, that explained to her cis-gender peers what life as a trans teen was like. "Navigating High School as an LGBTQ Teen" was watched by over half a million people, and "Ten Things You Didn't Know About Transgender People" had almost 250,000 views within two weeks!

WORKBOOK

1. Can you get your hands on a smartphone to video your script?
If yes, continue. If no, write your script and disseminate it to friends and family in the event that its genius will inspire someone to lend you a device that will let you shoot your video.

2. Now think of what you want people to know. Robby's videos are so watchable because he is funny (and a great dancer!), but he also advises us how to be respectful, converse with an open mind, and approach life with joy.

3. How do you want to communicate your message? A song? A play?

4. Enlist friends! Your video will be better if it's collaborative. And everything is more fun with friends.

5. Where will you post your masterpiece once it's done? Possibilities include YouTube, Tumblr, Facebook, or your own personal blog. Make sure there is no personal information (address, email address or phone number) in the video before you post it on a public site, and check your privacy settings. ou could also send it to someone else's channel or page. Ask them first!

11) PERFORM GUERRILLA THEATRE

Guerrilla theatre is not an event with large hairy animals. It is a staged political spectacle, often in the outdoors, often in the form of a play or a dance, often humorous. **Tessa Rose-Scheeres**, ten, saw the power of guerrilla theatre when she watched, via the internet, a group of almost two hundred Hillary Clinton supporters run from all directions into New

NOT THIS SORT OF GORILLA!

York City's Union Square. They wore colourful trouser suits as homage to their presidential candidate's fashion style and, much to the surprise of onlookers, suddenly burst into a joyous and energetic dance. The choreographer later explained to the media that the dance moves included lifting their faces to the sun to indicate renewable energy, and raising fists in unison to support #blacklivesmatter.

The effect was at once disruptive, uplifting, and inspirational. "It looked like everyone was having fun and also expressing their inner thoughts and beliefs," Tessa said, and decided that she could organize a group of kids to do the same thing. She put the word out, but when only a few showed up to the first practice, Tessa redoubled her efforts. She approached her friends with Post-it notes, asking them to invite three more friends. "I told them we were going to dance to save the world!" Tessa explained. Soon twenty-three kids were rollicking to Tessa's choreography and searching for trouser suits in charity shops.

On the appointed day they gathered at a central location in Berkeley, California, and, as a large speaker blasted music, they let loose in favour of renewable energy, women's rights, and racial equality. Their dance routine was met with cheers and live applause. To spread their message, they posted a video on the internet, widening their audience and increasing their own fun (see **Use Social Media** on page 52)! They had also alerted the media, so the participants were interviewed by television reporters and appeared on local news shows that evening.

Slam poetry, drums, Aztec dance, and your hip-hop band all have a place in guerrilla theatre! Don't like what your local council is doing? Write some rap lyrics, grab a milk crate and some friends, and perform on the pavement outside your town hall.

WORKBOOK

1. You probably won't find it difficult to think up hilarious, disruptive spectacles, because you're a kid, and you're excellent at that. Staging a pillow fight on a street corner sounds amusing. So does throwing water balloons from moving unicycles. But do those actions make important points beyond "I am super annoying"? (No.) Guerilla theatrics relay a social message, and they should also be fun for the people around you.

Take some time to think this through. Pick your cause, and write down aspects of that cause you think are vital. For instance, Hillary supporters knew that she wore colourful trouser suits. They also wanted to highlight her point of view (and theirs) on issues like climate change and equality. What do you want to highlight?

2. What talent of yours could lead to a public performance? Can you write a play or a song? Do you sing or dance? Are you good at making costumes? Are you a mime artist? Do you cartwheel with grace? Or do you have friends whose talents you can marshal?

3. Tessa drew inspiration from guerrilla theatre that someone else created, and then organized her own action. So scour the internet for examples that inspire you! Riff on other people's ideas. Be sure to give them credit, if possible.

4. Enlist friends!

5. Practise your event. While guerrilla theatre often looks spontaneous, it has usually taken many hours of work and refinement.

6. When you're ready, pick a place to perform. You will want to draw a crowd. Tessa says that it's best to find a street closed to traffic, or block out a space beforehand. Sometimes you may even need to apply for a street permit.

7. Alert the media.

8. Video your performance (see **Use Social Media** on page 52).

9. Have fun.

12) BE THE MEDIA

Carmen Hedrick, ten, **Lucy Newsom**, ten, and **Leah Brown**, eleven, wanted kids to have a voice, so they started a neighbourhood newspaper, all by themselves. They wrote the articles, the recipes (for chocolate-covered bacon), and the horoscopes (Cancer: purple polka-dotted hippos will lick your feet on a Wednesday night!), and they drew their own comic section. These were then cut out and glued onto new paper, copied at the local office supply store, and then bound by rubber bands. Voilà! The first issue of the *Lindley Park Gazette* was completed!

Soon over three hundred people were reading the free newspaper, which was delivered by bicycle or obtained from a pavement newspaper box. Local businesses paid five dollars to advertise in each issue, and this covered printing costs. Eventually there was a staff of over twenty-five kids! Articles included anything of interest to young people, like the increase of flying bats in the neighbourhood, or the St. Patrick's Day Parade. But the newspaper also took strong stands.

Before a statewide election that included an attempt to ban gay marriage, the *Lindley Park Gazette* journalists wrote an editorial that called this amendment "bullying." They asked their readers to vote no, since they, as kids, couldn't vote themselves.

> **We believe that gay marriage is fine. It is cool with us. But more than that, no matter how you feel about gay people, bullying is never OK. Never. We pledge to stand up for the people who are getting bullied, no matter who they are. We will not let the bullies win on the playground or in our government. Please VOTE (for us) AGAINST AMENDMENT ONE.**

Unfortunately the amendment against gay marriage passed, but the *Lindley Park Gazette* had made itself heard loud and clear (see **Go to It!** on page 106)!

Kids can also make their voices heard over the radio! **Youth Radio** offers six months of instruction to youth between fourteen and twenty-four years old. They learn how to interview, write, record, edit, and produce radio shows. These shows have been broadcast on National Public Radio stations across the United States, and heard around the world. Reports are often very personal and include stories on bullying, teen suicide, and foster care.

Other media outlets include zines, blogs, podcasts, online newspapers, and magazines!

WORKBOOK

1. What media suits you best? Radio, newspapers, blogs, video blogs, and zines can all be considered media.

2. Are you going to start something on your own, like the young editors of the *Lindley Park Gazette* did? Or will you join an organization that helps you put out your work, like Youth Radio?

3. Gather friends with skills that go beyond the ones you have!

4. Will your endeavour be cost-free (like a blog), or will you have to raise money for printing or equipment?

5. Commence!

ACTIVIST TIP INTERSECTIONALITY

It's easy to see people just one way.

But everyone has many identities.

OUR VOICES MATTER

DEAR MR. PREZ.

These identities intersect to form a unique life experience, with differently weighted privileges and disadvantages. This is called **intersectionality**.

Intersectionality acknowledges that, for example, the sexism you experience as an American Muslim girl cannot be understood without looking at attitudes toward Muslims in America, just as the sexism you as a white girl experience cannot be assessed without understanding the privilege that comes with being white.

Understanding which identities offer privilege and which don't and how these identities intersect is vital because overlapping identities form unique social justice situations. To get a better sense of this, write down your many identities. There are more than you think! Race, nationality, gender, looks, health, wealth, education, sexual orientation, immigration status, age, and religion are some examples of those commonly tied to social justice situations. Assess the ways each identity has an impact on your daily life, and then how they combine to make up the you that is You.

13) WRITE A BOOK

Books are a powerful way to educate people about a cause, because they explain your message through a story. Who doesn't love a story, right?

Nancy Yi Fan was in her sixth-grade social studies class when she learned about the 9/11 terrorism attacks that led to four plane crashes that brought down the World Trade Center, damaged the Pentagon, and killed thousands of people. That night she had a terrible dream about warring bird clans. She decided to spread a message of world peace by writing a book based on the nightmare. It took guts and hard work, but *Swordbird* was finished a year later. *Swordbird* debuted on the *New York Times* bestseller list, and since then Nancy has written two more books in the series.

Remember, the sentences in your story might not actually say, *Hey, people, (Major Injustice here) is going on and we must stop it!* Instead, the ideas behind your cause can be represented in the dialogue, action, and characters that you create. Nancy's Swordbird books are a call for world peace, but her stories are about clans of birds and martial arts!

WORKBOOK

1. Writing takes practice, long hours, and hard work. You in? Good.

2. Will you be writing a short story or a long book?

3. Set a deadline!

4. Write.

5. Keep writing.

6. Edit.

7. Share with friends and get feedback. Are your themes clear? Does the story move quickly?

8. *Write more.*

9. Edit more.

10. Write "The End."

11. Get it out there! Remember, you don't have to sell your book to a publishing house to make a difference. Your stories can be distributed to friends and family using the internet. You can also print them onto paper yourself, clip the papers together, draw a cover, and voilà, you have a book! If you want to get really fancy, you can see if a company online will do that for you, but that will mean saving a lot of your pocket money.

14) INVENT SOMETHING

If the change you are looking for doesn't exist, do what great minds (and hearts) like yours do: invent that change yourself!

Lalita Prasida Sripada Srisai of India knew that dirty drinking water was a big problem in her village, so when she was just eleven she dropped a dried corncob into a glass of murky water, wondering if it could absorb contaminants. Sure enough, the water quickly became much clearer. Corncobs are discarded into large piles on the side of roads and fields where Lalita lives, so when Lalita built a water purification system with them, she was also putting vast amounts of waste to good use. Lalita showed that these readily available cobs could filter out almost 80 per cent of the detergents, oils, mud, fertilizer, and pesticides found in ponds and streams near her home. While the water wasn't pristine, it became usable for things like washing and watering, saving valuable fresh water for drinking! Lalita sees a future where these simple, cheap filter systems can be installed in homes. She also envisions an easy way to clean up local

ponds — fixing multiple corncobs along the length of bamboo poles and lowering them into the water to continually absorb contaminants!

Ann Makosinski, fifteen, had a friend in the Philippines who did not have electricity in her home, and couldn't do her homework after dark. Ann knew that warmth radiates off our human skin with enough energy to activate a 100-watt light bulb, so she invented a flashlight powered from the heat of the hand that holds it! In one fell swoop Ann created a cheap and reliable light source, kept corrosive batteries from landfills, and helped a friend.

If you're not science minded, you can still create something new that changes the world for the better. **Leah Nelson**, ten, decided that being nice was powerful. So she started a campaign called Becuz I Care, which encouraged people to perform small acts of kindness for one another. Leah knew that it wasn't enough just to say, "Hey, let's be super friendly, people! The world will be a better place!" Instead she invented a game where one person performs a nice deed for someone else, and then hands her a bracelet, saying something like, "In a world with so many issues, let's just show other people that they are valued." The person receiving the bracelet then performs an act of generosity towards someone else, and passes the bracelet, and the sentiment, on. Leah's invention was brilliant! She used the old-fashioned game of tag to invent a new way to distribute kindness.

Marley Dias, eleven, was a big reader, but she couldn't find books that featured black girls like her. Were these books out there, or were the local schools and libraries just not interested in acquiring them? She set a goal: find a thousand such books. She called her campaign #1000blackgirlbooks, and took to social media for suggestions and donations. Marley exceeded her dream (four thousand books and counting!), AND she increased awareness of how few books in school libraries and classrooms reflect the lives of people of colour. Now she's written a book of her own, called *Marley Dias Gets It Done: And So Can You!*

WORKBOOK

1. What is missing in the world? Lalita thought it was a simple, cheap, accessible way to purify water; Ann thought it was reliable light; Leah thought it was kindness; and Marley thought it was representation of lives like hers in libraries and school curriculums.

2. Brainstorm ideas! Then consider your special skills. That may be tree climbing, singing, electronics, or illustration.

3. Can you create something pairing your special skill with what you feel is missing in the world?

4. Great. Now write down everything you'll need, and who will help you.

5. Consider how you will get your invention into the world and share it with others.

6. Take your invention and your plan to the person(s) in step 4 and talk to them about what you should do next.

7. Get to work!

15) TAKE THEM TO COURT

Why not fight for justice in the halls of justice? Don't just march up to the steps of the courthouse – march right in!

This is what the **"climate change kids"** are doing. Twenty-one young people are currently suing the United States government and the president, arguing that extreme weather disasters violate their constitutional right to liberty and property, and demanding that the government enact policy to radically reduce polluting emissions. Ten-year-old **Levi Draheim** lives on a small island off the coast of Florida. Sea level rise will obliterate his home, and the increased heat is already destroying surrounding coral. "A couple of our reefs . . . they're just almost gone. I can't even go to the beach. It gives me nightmares," he told the media.

Using the law to further your cause is smart! Policy changes by governments and companies have a big impact. But lawsuits require a lot of money, much more than your allowance, even in your wildest dreams. The climate change kids are being guided by adults, many who are scientists and lawyers. If you have some scientists and lawyers in your life, or can enroll a few talented adults to your cause, then by all means consider using the law to change the world.

WORKBOOK

1. Is the injustice you're concerned about also illegal? (Dumping toxins in rivers, adding addictive chemicals to cigarettes, paying workers below minimum wage.)

2. Research this! You may have to ask adults for help, because laws are complicated.

3. Is there currently a case in the legal system that fights your fight? If so, what can you do to help? (See **Volunteer!** on page 21; **Raise Money** on page 25.)

4. Is there a way for you to publicize the illegal activity, even if you don't have the funds to actually go to court? (See **Use Social Media** on page 52 and **Be the Media** on page 64.)

ACTIVIST TIP DIRECT ACTION

It's fine to ask for change, and it's fine to discuss change, but sometimes people feel they need to demand change. Activists demand change through **direct action**. Direct actions are those actions that defy expected customs and rules, and that challenge authority and "business as usual." They include strikes, blockades, walk-outs, and sit-ins. Direct action is used after many of the conventional ways (changing habits, letter writing, speaking face-to-face, and going to court, for example) have not worked.

Sometimes, but not always, a direct action entails deliberately and ethically breaking the law. This is also called **civil disobedience**. Activists break a law when they believe they are upholding a higher *moral* law.

Be aware that a direct action can put people at odds with police. This can be very dangerous, and it is not a situation to be taken lightly.

16) MARCH

Walking the streets with a group of people, often while chanting, singing, and waving a sign (see **Make a Protest Sign** on page 8), is a powerful way to fight injustice. This is called a protest march, and can be considered a direct action. It is not to be confused with marching out of a room because you are upset with your little brother. That is simply called "being mad."

The Women's March was a protest that called for women's rights and took a stand against the newly installed US president Donald Trump, who had spewed sexist and racist statements during his campaign. **Mari Copeny**, nine, of Michigan, participated because she "wanted to be one of the hundreds of thousands of voices showing what girl power is about." Mari knew how mighty people were when gathered together in protest. In fact, millions (yes, with an *m*!) of women and men, girls and boys, joined the Women's March in their towns, cities, and capitals. There were marches on all seven continents, from Nigeria to Lithuania to Antarctica!

In 1963, young African Americans marched peaceably in the streets of Birmingham, Alabama, to protest against violence, racism, and segregation. They were told to disperse because they were "parading without a permit." But these participants in what became known as the **Children's Crusade** marched on and were arrested by the hundreds during the next few days. The police also aimed fire hoses and set attack dogs on the marchers, so that the very racism and violence the kids were protesting was captured by newspapers and TV and shown around the world, causing an international outcry. This pressured Birmingham officials to release the jailed young protesters and begin to dismantle their racist laws and practices. At the time there were no black firefighters, police officers, bus drivers, or shop workers in Birmingham. The city's cinemas and buses had separate seating for blacks and for whites, and many restaurants and community pools were for whites only.

The Children's Crusade showed that breaking the law for social justice can be very effective. But it showed that it can also be very dangerous, especially for people from some racial groups, and sadly this continues to be true today.

WORKBOOK

1. Are you joining a march? Make sure you understand the mission of the march, and that it aligns with your own concerns. You must also speak to your parents and get their permission to join the march. (They may even march with you!)

2. Make sure your cause is clear and you know what you're trying to say. Are you protesting about polluted streams near your home? Are you marching to save your local hospital? Are you protesting about racism? Are you protesting about an unfair law?

3. Get ready with your protest sign, a few rhyming chants, and your friends. If you're joining a big march, your group could highlight your age so that people know that kids are involved and that you have an opinion. For example your placards could shout 'Kids demand Equal Rights for All' or express your worries about what adults are doing to your world.

4. Gather friends and parents to join you (see **Use Social Media** on page 52).

5. If you are organising your own march, you need to follow the rules. In the UK, you need to tell the police in writing the date and time of your march, the route, and the names and addresses of the organisers, at least six days in advance. Marches often begin or end at a place of significance to the cause, such as a government building.

6. Inform the media!

7. Gather speakers who will explain the issue and inspire the crowd.

8. Draw your protest sign (see **Make a Protest Sign** on page 8).

9. Will your clothing make a statement, too? At the Women's March, many people also wore pink hats to signify their solidarity to women's rights (see **Perform Guerrilla Theatre** on page 59).

10. Write the phone number of a responsible adult or parent on your arm in case you are separated. Marches can be chaotic.

11. Pack snacks and water.

12. Got drums, a saxophone, or a whistle? Bring them!

13. March!

ACTIVIST TIP

PROTEST CHANTS:

WHAT DO WE WANT?

PEACE!

WHEN DO WE WANT IT?

NOW!

THE PEOPLE, UNITED, WILL NEVER BE DIVIDED!*

SHOW ME WHAT DEMOCRACY LOOKS LIKE!

THIS IS WHAT DEMOCRACY LOOKS LIKE!

*INCLUDE DRUMS FOR BEST EFFECT.

17) WALK OUT

On the lookout for cool new shoes to walk in? Great. But make sure they're comfortable, because you may want to wear them for walkout-ing, too.

Students all around the United States walked out of their schools to protest about the 2016 election of President Trump. Carrying signs or making statements to the media, they decried his mistreatment of women, the multiple times he had reportedly failed to pay workers, the many well-documented falsehoods, his refusal to release his tax forms, and his bigoted immigration policies. **Hebh Jamal**, a public high school student in New York City, told the media, "We can't go to school, to class, to our exams as if things were normal." **Milan Matthes-Kale**, fifteen, said that she was scared for her future, and that adults had let her generation down by electing Trump, so "it's our job to fix it now, since they clearly can't get their act together." Walkouts are a direct action.

Hundreds of students from **Forest Grove High School** in Oregon stood up and left their classes after an anti-immigration sign was hung anonymously in the school hall. Word quickly spread through social media, and soon nearby middle school and high school kids left their schools as well. These students weren't ditching class for fun. They were staging a walkout. Upset about the banner and previous bigoted incidents at Forest Grove High School, all the students marched to the school district office to demand that the board take bigotry and intolerance seriously.

A well-planned walkout disrupts the daily routine. Imagine if school buses stopped in front of your school as usual, but before you and your friends could get on, the bus drivers stood up from their seats, removed their driving gloves, made their way down the steps, and marched off. You'd be curious to know what they were protesting about, right? (Especially because now you are stuck at school.)

One person can perform a walkout, but I'm sorry to say that, as well-dressed, funny, and dynamic as you may be, when you get up and leave alone, your protest will probably go unnoticed. However, when tens, hundreds, *thousands* of people walk out in a coordinated manner, it's hard not to get the message: something important is at hand. This is why getting people to work together as one is so effective! The New York students couldn't vote yet, but by leaving their classrooms in great numbers, they could proclaim their disgust over Trump's policies and their disappointment with voters.

In 2018, students across the United States participated in walkouts to show support to victims of school gun violence and to protest what they saw as a lack of progress in addressing this important political issue.

The first major walkout took place on March 14, exactly one month after a mass shooting at Marjorie Stoneman Douglas High School. Students from Stoneman Douglas organized the walkout, taking to social media to spread the word. Students across the nation left classes for seventeen minutes, one minute representing each student who had died at Stoneman Douglas.

A second major walkout took place on April 20, which was the anniversary of the 1999 Columbine High School shooting where two gunmen shot thirteen students before turning their guns on themselves. Students participating in this protest wore bright orange, the same color that hunters use to make themselves known to other shooters in the woods.

Between both events, thousands of students used the power of stepping away from the classroom to send a clear message: with students' lives at stake, gun control matters now.

18) JUST SIT DOWN

Hundreds of students at **Albany High School** in California held a sit-in to protest against classmates whose recent social media posts included mockery of female students for their race and weight, comments about slavery, and photos of the white supremacist group the Ku Klux Klan. Outraged youth began their three-hour sit-in outside the building's front doors, while inside the people responsible for the hateful messages met with teachers and classmates. Holding signs that read **Black is Beautiful** and **We Won't Stand for Racism**, protesters eventually spread out around the perimeter of the school. The sit-in forced the offenders to slink out a back entrance, even as their fellow students rushed to confront them.

Tenzin Norsang, whose sister had been one of those bullied on the posts, told the media, "I want them to face what they did and the effect they've had on the community."

The Albany High students dispersed once the offending classmates had left the grounds, but it does not always end that way. Sometimes sit-in

participants refuse to move, and if that happens there's a good chance someone is going to move you anyway. This is what happened to fifteen-year-old **Claudette Colvin** in Montgomery, Alabama, in 1955 when she was

ordered to give up her seat on the bus to a white woman, and refused. "It's my constitutional right to sit here as much as that lady. I paid my fare," she is reported to have said. The police pulled her from the bus and took her to jail, and she was eventually convicted of disturbing the peace, breaking the segregation law, and assault. But her sit-in inspired the famous civil rights activist Rosa Parks to refuse to move from her own bus seat later that year.

If you refuse to leave when asked by the police to do so, you are now breaking the law. Sit-ins can end in arrests. This is both a powerful statement and a reason to think very, very, very, very carefully before using this tactic, not to mention a reason that a sit-in will be a hard sell with your parents.

As Claudette was well aware, sit-ins can be *extremely* dangerous, especially if you are a person of colour. Sadly, it is likely that some children may have an easier time if the sit-ins lead to police action.

WORKBOOK

1. Why is a sit-in the best tactic for your cause?

2. Have you tried other tactics? Sit-ins are often escalations. Activists join together to sit in when nothing else has worked.

3. What are your privileges (are you white, rich, related to someone in government)? What privilege do you lack (are you brown, with less money)? Consider these before embarking on any action that could lead to confrontations with police.

4. Where should you sit in? Are you blocking something (people going to work, horses from going into the rodeo ring) or making a symbolic gesture (sitting on the steps of a public building, but letting people pass)?

5. Will friends be joining you? Can you trust them to watch out for you?

6. Alert the media. The more people who hear about your sit-in, the more your cause will catch on.

7. When/if you are asked to disperse, will you? Have you made your point loud and clear without tangling with the police (hopefully, yes).

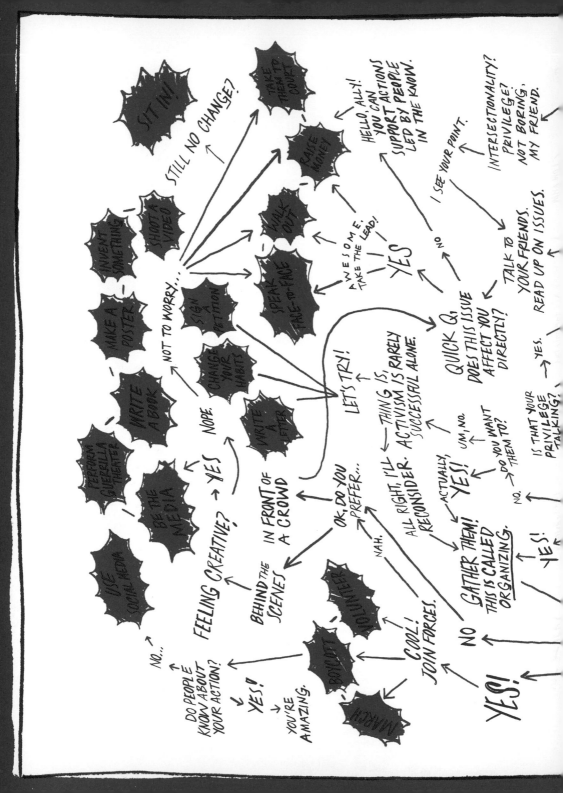

WHAT TACTIC SHOULD I USE?

DO YOU UNDERSTAND YOUR CAUSE?

YES / NO

ACTUALLY, I KNOW IT ALL.

PRIVILEGE.

EXACTLY.

NO PROBLEM. WILLING TO DO RESEARCH?

WILL DO!

WHY NOT?

NO.

COOL! DO MORE RESEARCH. WE NEVER KNOW ENOUGH.

SOUNDS AWESOME! WILL FRIENDS JOIN YOU?

ARE OTHERS ALREADY WORKING ON THIS ISSUE?

STRONG ACTIVIST ROOTS

BELIEF IN ONESELF

SENSE OF PURPOSE

PASSION FOR JUSTICE

READINESS TO TAKE ACTION

19) GO TO IT!

This final tactic isn't really a tactic at all. It's just a hallelujah, a congratulations-you've-finished-this-book, and a call to action, all rolled into one. You've seen how other kids have changed the world. Now it's your turn.

This book is an instruction manual, and instruction manuals come with a warning (do not overcharge battery, use only with a helmet, may explode

upon impact). This one is no different.

Yes, change takes time. It's often built using small actions the size of snowflakes. Put enough snowflakes together and – voilà! – you've got yourself an awesome snow sculpture (and, hopefully, a snow day).

THE SNOWBALL EFFECT!

Okay, it's time to get out there. Grab your friends. Talk these tactics over with them. Consider which ones inspire, but also consider which ones work best for the justice you are fighting for in the world. Now take action! Don't forget to throw on your superhero capes (and your snow boots).

Together you will change the world.

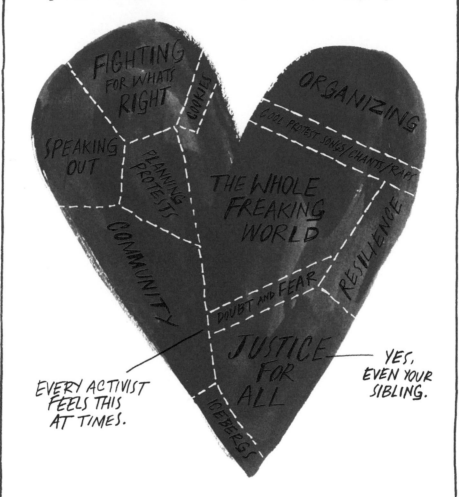

HEART OF AN ACTIVIST *

FIGHTING FOR WHATS RIGHT

ORGANIZING

COOKIES

COOL PROTEST SONGS/CHANTS/RAPS

SPEAKING OUT

PLANNING PROTESTS

THE WHOLE FREAKING WORLD

RESILIENCE

COMMUNITY

DOUBT AND FEAR

JUSTICE FOR ALL

ICEBERGS

EVERY ACTIVIST FEELS THIS AT TIMES.

YES, EVEN YOUR SIBLING.

* STUDIES SHOW IT IS *BIGGER* THAN AVERAGE.
** BEATS PER MINUTE: SIMILAR TO THE BEAT OF YOUR OWN DRUM.

READING LIST

For more inspiring stories of how kids have changed the world — and advice on how you can, too — check out these books.

Marley Dias Gets It Done: And So Can You! by Marley Dias

We Will Not Be Silent: The White Rose Student Resistance Movement That Defied Adolf Hitler by Russell Freedman

Claudette Colvin: Twice Toward Justice by Phillip Hoose

March (the trilogy) by John Lewis

Turning 15 on the Road to Freedom: My Story of the 1965 Selma Voting Rights March by Lynda Blackmon Lowery

The Help Yourself Cookbook for Kids: 60 Easy Plant-Based Recipes Kids Can Make to Stay Healthy and Save the Earth by Ruby Roth

Be a Changemaker: How to Start Something That Matters by Laurie Ann Thompson

Politics for Beginners by Alex Frith, Rosie Hore and Louie Stowell

People of Peace: Meet 40 amazing activists by Sandrine Mirza and Le Duo

Fantastically Great Women Who Changed The World by Kate Pankhurst

ACKNOWLEDGMENTS

Changing the world is a group effort, and so is writing a book! Many thanks to the political and tactical wisdom of Ashley Antoinnette Allen, Charlotte Davis, Pam Harris, Courtney Martin, Alexandra Paul, Shanell Williams, and Stephanie Yazgi.

Thank you, Lauren Tamaki, for freaking fantastic illustrations.

Thank you, Charlotte Sheedy, Nancy Miller, and Susan Dobinick for all the work you've done to put this book into the world.

Thank you to my twin, Alexandra, and my brother, Jonathan. You are inspirations to activists everywhere, and true north to my moral compass.

Thank you, San Francisco Writers' Grotto. Community is essential!

Thank you, Wendy.

A NOTE ON THE AUTHOR AND THE ILLUSTRATOR

Caroline Paul is the author of the *New York Times* bestselling *The Gutsy Girl: Escapades for Your Life of Epic Adventure* as well as the adult titles *Lost Cat: A True Story of Love, Desperation, and GPS Technology*; *East Wind, Rain*; and *Fighting Fire*. She lives in San Francisco, California.

carolinepaul.com

@carowriter

Lauren Tamaki has illustrated for many publications, including the *New York Times*, *New York* magazine, and the Brooklyn edition of the Wildsam Field Guides. *You Are Mighty* is her first children's book. She is from Canada and currently lives in Brooklyn, New York.

laurentamaki.com

@laurentamaki

Instagram: laurentamaki